BASIC METHODS FOR WORKING WITH FOIL

Aluminum foil makes it easy to create special decorations in your home. Here are some of the basic techniques devised for working with the versatile material:

PLEATING Accordion-pleated aluminum foil is needed for several of the designs in this book. It is simple to do and makes the foil stronger for forming large figures. To pleat, tear a sheet of foil of the desired length from the roll. Lay the sheet on a flat surface and fold over about an inch of the foil, beginning at one lengthwise edge of the foil. Now, double this folded portion back against the foil sheet, creasing foil to form another fold. Repeat this process, folding back and forth, until entire sheet is pleated.

CRUSHING Crushed foil can be used to make wreaths, letters, small animals, and many other ideas given in this book. Crushing is the basic operation for making the large animals in Conny's Zoo. Beginning with a sheet of foil, crush lightly with the hands along the lengthwise direction. This light crushing can result in circles of foil for various decorations, long ropes of foil, or narrow foil for forming letters.

COVERING Ordinary drinking straws covered with aluminum foil can make delightful mobiles and table decorations when combined with artificial flowers or nuts. A piece of aluminum foil about 2 inches long will cover a straw. Simply lay the foil on a flat surface, place straw on top of long edge, and roll straw, taking foil along with it. A group of these foil-covered straws, tied or wired together at the center, can be formed into a lovely starburst effect. Boxes of all types can be covered with aluminum foil. Cover top and bottom separately for smooth appearance and reusability of the gift container. Designs of colored tape, construction paper, poster paint can be used to "dress up" an ordinary box covered with foil.

MOLDING An almost unending number of shapes can be created by molding several layers of aluminum foil over an object of desired form. When removed, the foil retains the shape of the object. This technique will produce a bell by shaping Alcoa Wrap over a custard cup or bell-shaped glass. A reflector star can be molded using a common star-shaped candle holder.

FORMING CONE Cones are used in many of the designs in this book. They are easy to make and can be made of any desired size. Cut a circle of foil or paper and make a cut with scissors into the center. Now, form circle into a cone and hold with cellophane tape or glue.

MOLDING

FORMING CONE

COVERING

Alcoa's Book of Decorations

Decorations created by **Conny von Hagen**

•

Photographs by **Michael A. Vaccaro**

•

Illustrations by **William Dugan**

394.2

GOLDEN PRESS · NEW YORK

1959   95⊄

Introduction

Get set for Surprises in this book.

Look for light-hearted beasts and birds, never seen on land or sea.

Examine a glittering pleasure train that carries a covey of happy young passengers, yet never steams out of your living room.

Don't miss the radiant Christmas trimmings that you can assemble in your kitchen.

All these easy-to-make decorations were designed by Conny of Alcoa, pictured above with friend. Conny travels the country showing children and grown-ups how to make gay, lovely things of foil.

Decorations are like recipes — a family needs a variety for different situations. Some of the designs in this book are simple Quick Tricks; others are frankly Party, detailed and spectacular in effect. Every design is made with easily-available materials.

By all means, move over and let the children share in the art work. What if your first rabbit (page 60) does have a wobbly ear? Slight variations add charm.

The decorations on the following pages are for you to *make*, as well as to admire. Pull out your scissors and join the party!

CONTENTS

Christmas Is in Your Hands

Eager, busy hands make Christmas: hands rolling out cinnamon cooky dough, snipping fragrant pine boughs, wrapping presents, cutting a shining star for the tip of the tree. (*It's the loveliest Christmas tree we've ever had!*)

In this radiant, creative season, gifts and decorations made by hand seem especially appropriate. For one reason, most of the makings are right at hand during the holidays: ribbons, aluminum foil, stickers, decorative papers, plastic balls, ornaments, glitter dust. Foil gift-wrappings in brilliant colors have been used for several of the designs. These papers are also available at Christmas in art supply and variety stores and hobby shops.

Making simple decorations will keep children busy and happy on those feverish days right before Christmas. Even the smallest fingers can make the foil chain on the tree across the page or mold the tiny candy basket on page 10.

One of the precious gifts we offer to our friends at Christmas is our home, glowing with beauty and hospitality. The decorations shown here look inward and outward, delighting the family within the home and brightening the spirits of passers-by.

Look around you for furnishings to use as background for these sparkling holiday trims. Book shelf, bay window, or mantelpiece provide a delightful setting for the Silver Angels on page 17. Silver candlesticks, plus a cluster of the Choir Boys (page 19), combine in a distinctive centerpiece for dining table or buffet setting.

Select a few of these designs to add the holiday touch to candies, fruit, nuts, and evergreens. Tuck a covey of tiny birds (page 10) into a cluster of laurel or balsam for the mantelpiece. Offer wrapped candies on a Lollipop Wreath (page 26).

Most families treasure a holiday tradition that appears year after year until it is woven into the memories of the season. Your family signature could be the Nut Chain (page 12) for visitors to snip each year to find their fortune.

From Angel to Arturo (page 22), the *special* charm of these decorations is your personal gift of time and spirit.

Complete step-by-step directions for making tree decorations are shown on page 10.

CLUSTER OF STARS **1.** Make circle, about 3 inches in diameter. Cut slit to center. Cut six points. **2.** Tape or glue into cone shape. Stick pipe cleaner through center of each star. Glue small ornament to tip of pipe cleaner. **3.** Join stars together to form cluster.

BASKET **1.** Mold foil over custard cup or small gelatin mold (see front end papers). Remove from mold. Punch two holes for handle. **2.** Crush rope of foil (see front end papers). Stick one end of rope in one hole, pinch together, and do same with other hole.

BIRD **1.** Use 15-inch length of foil, plus two 1½-inch plastic foam balls. Place one ball in center of foil, the other at end. Roll foil the width of sheet, covering balls. **2.** Smooth foil over balls, crushing foil between balls. **3.** Lift ball forming head over body ball. Cut tail end of foil into three strips. Crush and twist into half circle. Glue on beak and crown (pattern on page 29).

STAR OUTLINE WITH LIGHT **1.** Form crushed foil (see front end papers) into five loops. **2.** Spread into star shape, attach to holder for tree light.

CLUSTER OF CIRCLES **1.** Cut several circles of foil, 2 inches across. Pinch foil at one side of circle, creasing foil to the center of the circle. **2.** Foil will resemble sketch. **3.** Join a series together by passing thread through points, pull together to form a cluster.

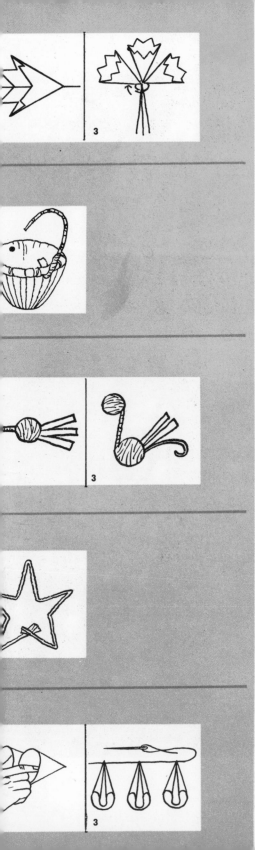

Especially for Children

Children love to feel themselves part of the bustle and excitement of getting ready for Christmas. Set aside a sturdy table or desk where your children can work away at cards, small gifts, and decorations. Since aluminum foil is clean, easy to handle, and inexpensive, it is a perfect art material for children.

A little assistance and encouragement will get your young artists off to a good start. Let them select two or three simple designs in this section, then help them with props or pattern. The basket on the opposite page, for instance, can be molded over a kitchen custard cup or muffin tin. It can be tied with bright ribbons and filled with tiny candies for a tree ornament. (Nice to give a favorite neighbor.) Drinking straws, covered with foil (front end papers) can be tied together with ribbon to form lovely star bursts to hang at door or window. Christmas boots (page 13) can be cut out by the youngsters, following a cardboard pattern, and stitched by older sister or Mother. Let the children decorate the boots with bright braid, bells, bows, initials in colored plastic tape. The boots, filled with scarf or gift hankies, would make a pretty gift for a teacher or favorite aunt.

Treasure Box of Trims Keep a family Treasure Box for collecting trimmings for the children to use on their foil artwork. An inexpensive clear plastic divided box, such as used for sewing equipment or fishing tackle, is excellent. Stash away bits of old jewelry, pearls, sequins, tiny shells, artificial flowers, sparkling buttons, one-of-a-kind earrings, veilings, gold braid, and feathers. Interesting trim adds magic to the simplest decoration.

Christmas Cards No matter how wobbly the angel or downhill the writing, every child's Christmas card is a triumph! Use stiff art paper or construction paper in bright colors for the cards.

Silver Angel Card: Cut out long cone shape of foil for body, add wings and head. Glue strands of glitter-string to head for hair. Add tiny foil stars to background.

Tree Card: Cut tree from foil and glue to dark green background. Trim tree with sequins, stars, circles. Sprinkle with glitter dust. Charming "family portrait" cards can be made from Christmas folders or holiday note paper. Instead of a written greeting, have the child paste in a snapshot of the family or children. Border the picture with frame of foil and sign names in crayon or colored pencil.

Gift Wrapping Save coffee cans, sturdy boxes, small plastic containers, even berry baskets to use as unusual Christmas gift containers. These containers can be decorated by the children and used to package gifts of home-made cookies, candies, and jellies. Berry baskets, for example, can be painted white, trimmed with holly, and lined with heavy-duty foil to hold almond nut cookies and fruit bars. Coffee cans are transformed into miniature travel cases (page 24) to hold small gifts, nuts, and candies. A shining bird (pattern on page 57) can be cut from foil by a child and used to decorate a gift box.

Under-the-Tree Town On page 37, photographs and descriptions are given for a Train Town, made from empty milk cartons, boxes, and cardboard. These same stores and houses can be made by children at Christmas for an under-the-tree town or as a station town for the electric train.

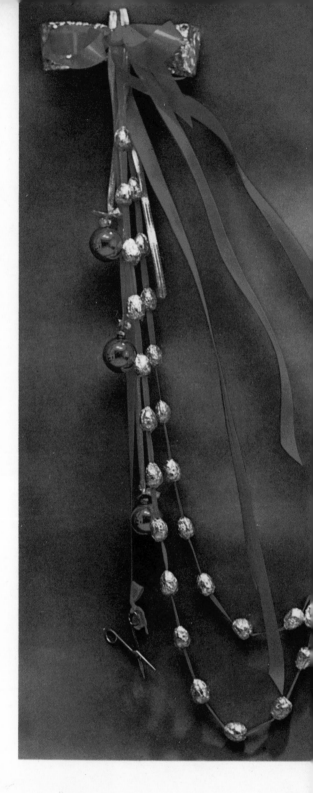

CHRISTMAS BOOTS Cut out boot or shoe shapes from double heavy-duty foil. Glue edges together or sew by machine, using widest stitch. Trim with ribbon bows, tiny bouquets, glitter braid, or paper cutouts. Stitch on loop of ribbon or braid to attach boots to mantel, table, or door. Personalize by adding names with felt-tipped color markers or with poster paint or with small figures such as those patterned on page 29. Boots can hold small gifts, cards. **Tip:** These bright boots make gay containers for Christmas gift hosiery, scarves, or lingerie.

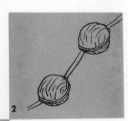

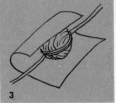

NUT CHAIN Mount this fascinating, old-world fortune chain on door or mantel to greet your guests. **1.** Carefully open 25 English walnuts, saving the nut meats for holiday cookies or candies. Slip into each opened shell a written Christmas wish, fortune prediction, or prayer. **2.** Close two halves of nut shells, with message and a portion of a long strip of ribbon inside. **3.** Cover each shell with aluminum foil. This holds the nuts together. Repeat this with remainder of shells, spacing them along the ribbon. Have visitors snip nuts to learn their fortunes.

STAR TREE This brilliant and unusual tree can stand in your living room, in a hallway, or on your porch to greet holiday callers. **1.** Form a tall cone (about 4 feet) of chicken wire. Slip cone over broomstick that has been anchored in a large flower pot or bucket with clay or sand. **2.** Thread Christmas tree light wires through the frame. **3.** Form foil stars by molding double-thick foil over an inverted star-shaped candleholder (see front end papers). Insert a light bulb through center of a foil star. Fill spaces between lights with additional foil stars.

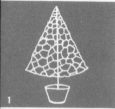

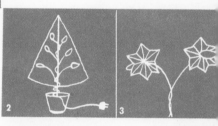

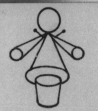

STARBURST MOBILE The glittering mobile at the left, gay with lovely flowers or Christmas tree ornaments, can be hung over a holiday table or in a window to catch the gleam from nearby lamp or candles. The bright rays spreading from the central globe are foil-covered drinking straws (see front end papers). **1.** Cover a 10-inch plastic foam ball with foil. Pin on artificial flowers. Insert foil-covered straws in holes punched with pencil point or ice pick. Gather 10 additional foil-covered straws. Pinch together at center and tie with thin wire. Spread straws to form starburst. Make several of these. **2.** Connect starbursts and ball with wire and hang.

SANTA CLAUS Here's an idea for gift-wrapping a jar of cookies or candies for someone special. Cover an empty coffee can or cottage cheese container with aluminum foil. Fit a red construction paper cone over container (see sketch above). Form two long, narrow cones of construction paper and tape to top of larger cone to form arms. Hands cut from construction paper are glued inside cone arms. Decorate figure with foil belt and crushed foil cuffs. A foam ball is the head. Decorate with face features of construction paper and a cotton beard. Hat is a cone of red crepe paper turned up to form a brim and bent down at the point. Feet (pattern page 29) are cut from black construction paper and glued to the underside of the container.

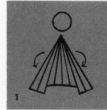

PLACE CARD ANGELS Tiny angels, such as those pictured on the left, make attractive holders of place cards for holiday dinner or party. **1.** Form cone from cardboard (see front end papers) and cover with foil. **2.** Crush foil (see front end papers) to form arms. Secure arms to back of cone with cellophane tape or glue. Top cone with foam ball. Complete head with angel hair and features. Tuck small place card into arms of angel.

PLACE CARD TREES For alternate place cards, use Christmas Tree stands topped with outline stars (pictured to the left). Cut three thicknesses of gift-wrap foil trees for each stand (pattern page 28). Fold in half. Staple trees together at fold and separate sections to stand upright. Add outline stars to top (pattern page 28).

SILVER ANGELS These messengers (at right) of the holiday season make beautiful table or mantel decorations. **1.** Pleat 3-foot length of 18-inch foil (see front end papers) and form into a cone. Cellophane tape will secure the top. Punch a small hole in a 3-inch plastic foam ball and slip ball over point of cone. **2.** Tape or glue wings and arms (patterns on page 28) to cone. **3.** Roll and pin foil hands around small birthday candles.

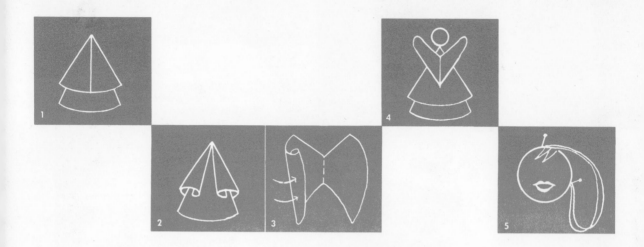

GOLDEN ANGELS Beautiful angels for table, window, buffet, or mantel are well worth the time to make. **1.** Make two cones of gold gift-wrap foil, one smaller than the other. Cut the smaller cone up the front and slip over the larger cone. **2.** Now, roll back the cut edges. **3.** Cut foil wings (pattern page 28). Roll each wing, as shown on photograph. **4.** Tape or glue wings to back of cone. **5.** Cut strips of foil for hair. Pin each strip to side of foam ball head. Bring strip ends up to top of head and pin.

CHOIR BOYS **1.** Form a cardboard cone and cover with foil (see front end papers). Crush foil and use for arms. Glue or tape arms to back of cone. **2.** Make a surplice from a paper doily, folded and slipped over top of cone. **3.** Top the cone with a plastic foam ball head. Add bow at neck. To make hair, cut out circle (pattern page 29) and snip edges to form shallow cone. Glue to head. Add features.

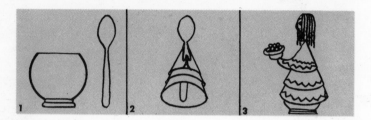

THREE KINGS These three gentlemen from The Christmas Story make fine table or mantel decorations. Here's how they are made: Left to right: **1.** The skeleton of the First King is a wooden spoon inserted in the opening of a small jar. The jar is filled with colored beads to hold spoon erect. **2.** Form three cones of colored foil, cutting each cone in an upswept line at the front. Decorate the bottoms with sequins and ric-rac. The cones should measure 4½, 5, and 5½ inches tall. (Hands are cut as a part of the smallest cone.) Cut a hole at the tip of of each cone and slip each one—beginning with the larger one—onto the handle of the wooden kitchen spoon. **3.** Now place the handle of the spoon into the small jar filled with beads. Place a small foil wreath in the hands and fill with beads and glitter. The head is the bowl of the spoon topped with shreds of foil or yarn for hair. **4.** The center King is a milk bottle with a red gift-wrap foil cone added. **5.** A black paper cape is cut in a cone shape to include arms. Glue a foam ball to the top of the bottle and add face features of felt or construction paper. **6.** Crush foil to the head for a turban. Balloon trousers of crushed foil cover the front and tuck up under the cape. Place a large bead or stone in the "hands" that are cut as part of the cape. **7.** For the Third King, slip a foil cone over the neck of a wine bottle. **8.** For the head, mold foil over a foam ball or small tree ornament and transfer to the top of the bottle, crushing foil where it overlaps ball around neck of the bottle. Raffia makes the hair, and the crown is cut from foil-covered construction paper or gift-wrap foil. (Camel is described on page 85.)

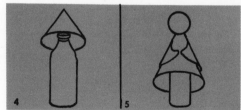

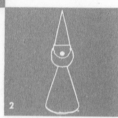

ARTUROS These delightful little gentlemen are easy to make. **1.** Assemble a 5-inch paper cone for the body and mount a small cone for a cap on a 2-inch diameter plastic foam ball head. Glue in place. Make cones from different colors of construction paper, covering one or two with Alcoa Wrap. **2.** Complete each Arturo by adding a holly berry nose and a beard of cotton. (The noses should be placed low, just above the cotton beards.) Add special features such as spectacles (pattern page 29) and mortarboard hat. Arturos can be used as place cards, favors, or in a group for table or mantel decorations.

ST. LUCIA ANGELS These gentle, wistful angels, named for the Swedish patron saint of Christmas, rest on the base of a foil-covered 4-ounce fruit juice glass. **1.** Cover fruit juice glass with foil. For body, make two cones of colored foil gift-wrap paper. First cone, to fit over foil-covered glass, should be approximately 7½ inches tall and just wide enough to fit over glass. Second cone should be 6 inches tall, to fit over first cone. **2.** Cut arms approximately 3½ inches long (pattern page 29). Cut wings from regular aluminum foil (page 28). **3.** Head can be either blown-out egg or egg-shaped plastic foam ball. Add some hair strands of colored paper. Glue head to body and add candle crown. Crown is small crushed wreath (see front end papers) with birthday candles.

HOLLY RING MOBILE This lovely and impressive mobile transforms any holiday table into a party scene. The mobile is made of five spheres or globes, each containing five crushed foil rings. **1.** For top sphere, make crushed foil ring 10 inches in diameter. Make each of the succeeding four rings a fraction smaller to nest inside the preceding ring. **2.** Spread rings to form spherical shape and tie at top and bottom, where they intersect, with string or thin wire. Start second sphere with 9-inch ring, third sphere with 8-inch ring, fourth sphere with 7-inch ring, and fifth sphere with 6-inch ring. Fasten all five globes together with single string or wire, fastening at both top and bottom of spheres. Decorate spheres with holly leaves, tree ornaments, mistletoe, evergreens, or Della Robbia fruits and nuts. Hang mobile from lighting fixture or ceiling.

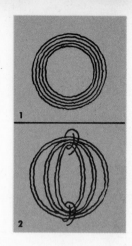

DISTINCTIVE GIFT WRAPPINGS Use household aluminum foil, plus a few ingenious tricks, to make the delightful gift wraps above, left to right. **1.** Felt Christmas trees and foil stars decorate flat box. **2.** Paper cup used for the tall hat on Calypso dancer. **3.** Coffee can, covered with foil, becomes a travel hat box. Use double-faced plastic tape for handle, add tiny travel stickers (page 28). **4.** Cone of gift wrap foil, trimmed with sticker stars and plastic tape, covers gift bottle. **5.** Reindeer head trim is plastic foam ball with ears and antlers of foil. **6.** Velvet rose contrasts with wrapping of textured foil. To texture foil: crumple gently in hand, then open and mold over package. **7.** Hand prints are bold decoration on large package. To make: outline hand on foil wrapping with crayon or grease pencil, fill in outline with poster paint. Add hand cutout of art paper for gift card.

SPARKLING WREATHS One of the most versatile indoor or outdoor decorations is the inexpensive foil wreath. It is shaped by crushing foil loosely into a wreath shape. A roll of heavy-duty Alcoa Wrap will produce one large wreath. Regular weight can be used for small ones. **1.** Roll out a long length of foil but don't tear off. Begin crushing this loosely along its length into a wreath shape of the desired size. **2.** Continue around the wreath again crushing another layer of foil (shiny side out) to it to add body. Continue adding layers until your wreath has sufficient body. Now tear off foil. **3.** Once made, the wreath can be decorated in many sparkling ways, such as:

LOLLIPOP WREATH Make a large wreath by crushing foil. An assortment of bright lollipops, as shown in the picture to the right, inserted in the wreath makes a gay greeting for children. Basic wreath can also be used for displaying greeting cards pinned to foil wreath.

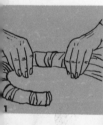

TREASURE TREE Here is a colorful, shiny tree that carries a cargo of candy and surprises for all. The actual tree shape is a large, 2-foot high cone shape, **(1)** made from light cardboard or heavy paper. It is covered with Alcoa Wrap, shiny side out. For the rings, make another cone, the same height but slightly fatter at the base. From this cone cut a 4- or 5-inch wide ring from the bottom. Then another ring of the same thickness and a third. Each of these three rings is covered with foil. **2.** Inverted, the rings are placed over the tree cone. The rings can then be filled with bright colored Christmas candy, small gifts or decorations to make a brilliant tree of sparkling colors.

DOOR WREATHS Foil wreaths lend themselves to an exciting number of attractive door decorations. As shown at right, three wreaths of successively smaller sizes are held together by loops of red ribbon. Large red bows decorate the top of each wreath.

WINDOW WREATH Inexpensive foil wreath is used as a window decoration in the sketch on the left below.

SNOW MAN A big foil snow man for your front yard is fun to make. Heavy-duty Alcoa Wrap is lightly crushed, then wound into a ball, just as snow is rolled onto a conventional snow man. As seen lower right, three such balls make the sparkling "foil man." When foil is loosely crushed together, two 25-foot rolls of heavy-duty should be enough to make a 5-foot man.

Wings
Page 23

Hatbox
Page 24

PARIS

Package
Page 24

Christmas Boot
Page 13

Ears
Page 19

Stars for Place Card Tree
Page 16

Eyebrows
Page 15

Place Card Tree
Page 16

Patterns are not necessarily to scale, but provided to give
you an idea of proper shape.

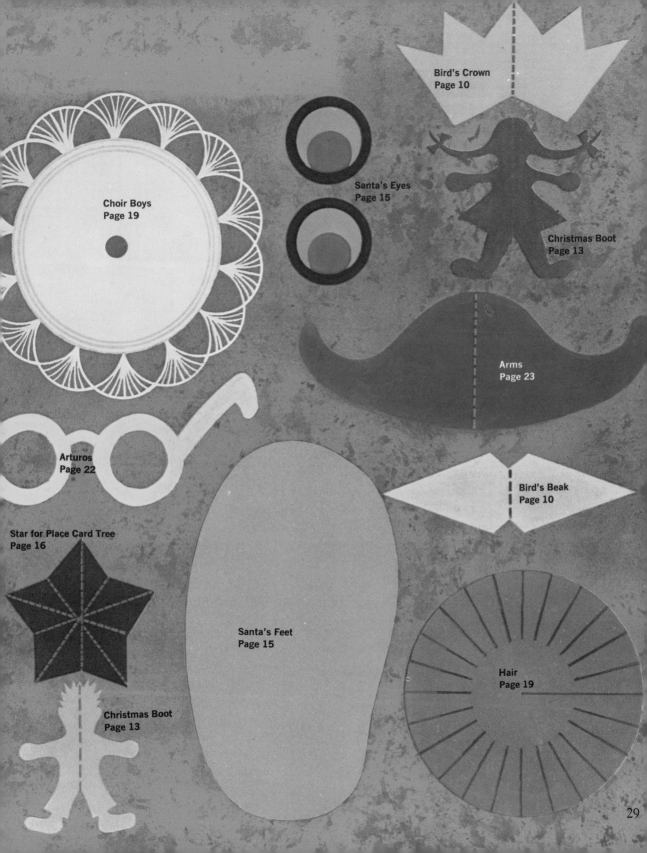

Bird's Crown
Page 10

Choir Boys
Page 19

Santa's Eyes
Page 15

Christmas Boot
Page 13

Arms
Page 23

Arturos
Page 22

Bird's Beak
Page 10

Star for Place Card Tree
Page 16

Santa's Feet
Page 15

Hair
Page 19

Christmas Boot
Page 13

29

Parties for Children

Parents often dream wistfully of the Perfect Party where children play quietly in an outdoor space, no one quarrels or spills lemonade, and the young guests all leave promptly in an hour.

But children's parties are usually livelier affairs, and the best preparation is plenty of rest and careful planning before the first small guests arrive.

A Few Party Rules   Here are some helpful suggestions culled from families with many service stripes in conducting successful children's parties:

• Decide on a time limit for the party and explain this to the young host or hostess and to parents of the young guests.

Preschool children	1½ hours
6 to 10	2 hours
10 to 12	3 hours

• Talk over plans of party with son or daughter. Let even the youngest child open door, greet guests, and accept gifts. Decide before the party when gifts shall be opened.

• Plan a few games suitable for the age of the guests. Have *plenty* of inexpensive prizes.

• Familiar food in fancy containers always makes a hit. Make use of disposable plates and cups, individually-packaged ice cream.

• A teen-age assistant is helpful on the scene to lead games, mop up spilled lemonade and help keep the party moving.

• All children sense the mood of the grownups at the party, so relax and enjoy the fun.

Any child walking into the gay setting shown across the page knows that fun and good times are on the way.

Here is a Circus Party, with crepe paper streamers festooned from an outdoor umbrella and a cargo of pretty balloons to take home as favors.

Under the striped tent is the Birthday Cake, decorated as a carousel. Another refreshment is the Clown Favor: the head is a juicy apple, the body a bottle of chilled soda pop. A circus horse on page 33 is the prize for the girl who won the peanut race!

But this is just the beginning of our junior party section. Chugging right ahead is the Train Party (pages 34 and 35), a surprise from conductor to caboose.

No special dress-up suits are needed for the Pirate Party on page 38. Let the boys come in sports shirts and slacks and make their own hats and cutlasses at the party.

If you have a camera, bring it out for the Space Party on page 39. The sight of six helmeted rocket men munching birthday cake should make a priceless picture. As a part of the fun, each boy can make his own helmet, with a prize for the best job.

All these easy-to-make party projects — circus horse, train, rocket helmet—have a happy bonus. They will provide many hours of entertainment for the children long after the party is over.

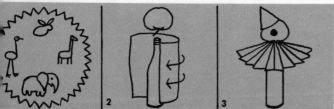

CIRCUS PARTY TABLE A delightful table is centered with a carousel cake. **1.** Place mats are circles of Alcoa Wrap cut out with pinking shears and decorated with animal stickers or stars. **2.** Delightful clowns are foil covered soda pop bottles with apple heads. Apples fit on bottle top by cutting small hole in bottom. **3.** Collar is made by accordion pleating colored foil gift wrap, and hat is paper cone covered with foil. **4.** Glasses are identified with card held on by toy plastic clothespins.

HOBBY HORSE A decorative prize for party games is this easy-to-make hobby horse. This equestrian delight is made from foil, a length of broomstick or 1-inch wooden dowel, and some ribbon, raffia or rug yarn. **1.** To make the horse's head, loosely crush foil into one 3-inch and one 4-inch ball. Mold additional sheets of foil over both of these balls and over the end of a 3-foot long wooden stick, shaping foil into the horse's head. (Details of simple techniques for sculpturing foil are on page 82.) **2.** Ears for the horse are cut from foil and glued in place. Eyes, nostrils, and mouth are cut from colored paper or felt and glued on. Harness is ribbon pinned or glued in place; and the hobby horse's mane can be ribbon loops, raffia, or yarn. To complete friend horse, cover the broomstick body with foil.

TRAIN PARTY When the young guests arrive, the train is waiting at the station with steam hissing and bell clanging ready for an exciting trip to Boston, Denver, Bombay, Cape-town, and points north, south, east, and west. A sparkling aluminum train provides a marvelous make-believe trip for the children. The train, made from boxes, foil, and foil pie plates, is ideal for four- to eight-year-olds. Here's how to make the train: **1.** The standard passenger car is a simple rectangular cardboard box covered with foil fastened to box with cellophane tape. Wheels are 9-inch foil pie plates painted black inside and glued to car. **2.** The big locomotive is made with a longer rectangular box. The curved hood on the top is a rounded square of cardboard. The front end is rounded with a crushed piece of Alcoa Wrap. All parts are foil-covered after assembling. Wheels are, again, pie plates. **3.** Cab for the locomotive is made from a square box with two sides removed and windows cut in for engineer. **4.** Stacks are red construction-paper cylinders held in place with tape. **5.** Front headlight is a small foil or paper plate, and the cowcatcher is foil-covered cardboard with stripes of red paper or plastic tape.

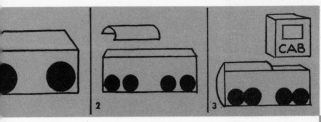

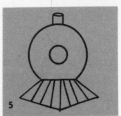

CAB

END OF THE LINE As the trip on the Choo-Choo Express begins to "lose steam" for the children, have the conductor call a stop at Toy City. This sparkling metropolis lies waiting on the dining room table surrounded by games and refreshments. This will keep the young guests busy and happy for another hour.

At the table, each place has a foil place mat decorated with a colorful train cut from construction paper. (Pattern page 57.)

The marker for each place is a small house made from foil-covered milk cartons. As shown below **(1)** the house has a construction-paper roof and **(2)** holds a balloon, crayons, favors and some colored pipe cleaners. All the contents can be used as props in creative games. First, with the crayons, have a drawing contest (paper for this can be placed under the foil place mat). Let the children judge and award a prize. Second, ask the guests to make an animal from the pipe cleaners with a prize for the best.

In the center of the Toy City is the birthday cake. If you can buy a miniature toy train at the 5 & 10, put it on the cake to hold the birthday candles. The rest of the city is a series of buildings made from boxes covered with foil and decorated. This gay village is an ideal project to keep your children busy getting ready for the party. Some ideas for buildings are shown in the sketches on the opposite page.

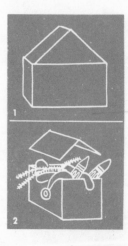

1. Food Shop is made from a foil-covered cleansing tissue box that has a rectangular opening on top (or cut such an opening). A store awning is cut from construction paper and given a scalloped edge and a sign, "Food Shop." (Some fruit can be put in the box as the food.) **2.** Bakery is another tissue box, covered with Alcoa Wrap, but this one has an oval opening on the side for the store window. **3.** Tall Tower for the town is made from the cardboard tube from an 18-inch wide roll of foil. The foil-covered tower has windows of construction paper pasted on and a roof made from a small cone of construction paper. **4.** Ice Cream Parlor is a foil-covered large can. Two ice cream cones are made from paper and glued on top. **5.** Church is a foil-covered shoe box with steeples made from two cardboard tubes from Alcoa Wrap or wax paper. Steeple roofs are cones made from construction paper.

PIRATE PARTY When your young Buccaneers arrive for the party, give each one an eye patch of black construction paper or felt and a bold hat with Jolly Roger insignia. Feed the Pirates at a table set with treasure-map place mats. Tear large sheets of construction paper into map shape, mark with secret code for treasure hunt after meal. Treasure chest on page 52 can be used as centerpiece. Scatter golden coins (foil-covered chocolate) over table. **Pirate Hats** are easily constructed from foil. **1.** First take two 24-inch long sheets of aluminum foil. Crush top and side together and spread bottom for head opening. Now place the partially completed hat over a child's head and crush it into the pirate hat shape. Remove the hat from child's head and using two more 24-inch long sheets of foil, crush one over either side of the hat to provide strength. **2.** The skull and cross bones is made using the pattern on page 56.

The Cutlass is just as easy to make as the hat. Crush a 3-foot long piece of heavy-duty Alcoa Wrap into the shape of the sabre shown being brandished at left. For the heavy end and knuckle guard add a 24-inch piece of foil. Crush the center 9 inches of the piece into the knuckle guard shape. Now crush the ends of the piece over the sword to hold in place.

A Pirate Ship is a delightful centerpiece for the pirate party. It can easily be made of foil. The hull of the ship is shaped from six 3-foot lengths of 18-inch-wide heavy duty Alcoa Wrap. Starting with one sheet, turn the edges up and begin shaping into a ship's hull. Continue adding the remaining pieces, gradually building up the hull. The masts are three 18-inch-long candles covered with foil. Foil is crushed around the bottom of each candle to make a base for them to stand in the hull. Sails are squares cut from foil and pinned on masts. Rigging made from string can be added.

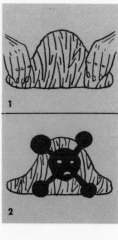

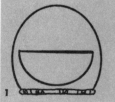

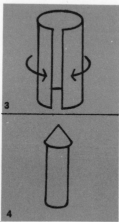

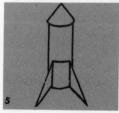

SPACE PARTY You can have a really happy bunch of children if you "blast-off" with a space party. All of the children can be given foil space masks and spend the party in a make-believe land of outer space. Instructions for making the basic mask shape of foil are on page 71. **1.** To adapt these general instructions to a sparkling space mask all the children will love, make the mask shape, skipping the process of adding a nose. Then cut a semicircle out of the lower half of the mask for the face opening. **2.** Add knobs made from paper cups or spools and antennae from crushed foil. These fixtures are attached with white glue.

An important attraction at a space party can be a shiny big rocket. **3.** This is easily made by making a cylinder of heavy paper or cardboard and a nose cone of the same material. **4.** Cover these with Alcoa Wrap to add a metallic sheen. **5.** The tail fins are based on the pattern on page 56. Again cut from cardboard, they are folded up along the dotted line. The rectangle between the dotted lines is the area glued to the rocket body. Using this general technique, you can make rockets as small as the one held by the spaceman in the photo above, or as large as your materials permit (5 feet or more).

Decorations for Special Days

What makes parties fun? Mood is the secret ingredient, the feeling of gaiety and anticipation that promises an occasion worth celebrating.

Broadway producers create this excitement by raising the curtain on a smash first-scene setting. A hostess establishes her party mood by greeting her guests in home or room decorated with flair and imagination.

The charming Valentine centerpiece on the opposite page, for instance, would start conversation in the opening minutes of a club luncheon. (The floral heart is made according to wreath instructions, page 26.) And any young bride would fondly remember her engagement party (page 52), decorated with a colorful floral wreath and gay, shining birds.

Since decorations are often last minute what-shall-we-put-on-the-table affairs, many of these ideas have been planned around objects at hand in the home. Bowls of fresh fruit are the base for the centerpieces on pages 44 and 45. Anyone with a pot of ivy or any other house plant can produce the Butterfly Tree on page 53. Even the branch of a tree can be converted into a centerpiece (page 55). All these gay eye-catchers are easy to make; all say, "Welcome to the party!"

VALENTINE CANDLESTICK   1. Join spout ends of two kitchen funnels by forcing one inside the other. Cover with foil. **2.** Place small foil pie plate or circle of heavy-duty foil on top of funnel-candlestick. **3.** Cut hole in plate and pass candle through. Candle is held upright in funnel by crushed foil. **4.** Heap artificial violets around candle. **5.** Tie velvet ribbon bow around candlestick.

Mother's Day

For Children Only If you are a mother, this section is not for you. Please turn the page quickly.

If you are a boy or girl able to use scissors or paper, gather around. Here's an idea for Mother's Day.

In the picture here, you see a new kind of bouquet you can make. These are not just ordinary flowers. Each blossom (made of colored facial tissues) is a Fortune Flower—Mother opens the paper and finds a message from you.

Your message can be a tiny picture or a poem or a promise to wash dishes for a week. Your brothers or sisters can add their messages, too.

If you are giving your mother another present, you can make a small bouquet with three or four flowers and fasten it on the gift box.

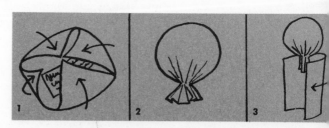

MOTHER'S DAY BOUQUET **1.** Write message or verse on small piece of paper. Enclose paper in middle of colored facial tissue. **2.** Pull up ends to form sack. **3.** Crush foil for stem, pinching about ½ inch of stem around base of sack to form flower. Gather a dozen flowers together and insert stems through hole in center of scalloped circle of foil to form nosegay.

Father's Day

Three cheers! At last a way to make something special of the necktie, socks, pipe, and slippers that Dad receives on Father's Day.

All the gifts are included in this easy-to-make figure to greet Dad when he enters the dining room. The king himself can be made in a few minutes from materials in your household. A broom forms head and body, a rubber ball provides the nose. Crown and ears are made of colored foil. Arms are crushed Alcoa Wrap. Gift scarf or sports shirt could be draped over the outstretched arm.

As a surprise for this happy day, have the artist in the family decorate a paper scroll. Write your thanks to Dad for his many kindnesses during the year—the times he has driven you to parties, the bike he fixed, the vacation he arranged. Or your scroll might be in the form of a giant Father's Day Card with verses and drawings from the entire family.

FATHER'S DAY FIGURE 1. Arms shaped from crushed foil are taped to broom handle and curved to the front. **2.** Pin a rubber ball nose, large foil ears, and a bright foil crown to broom. Gift pipe, tie, and slippers are added as shown.

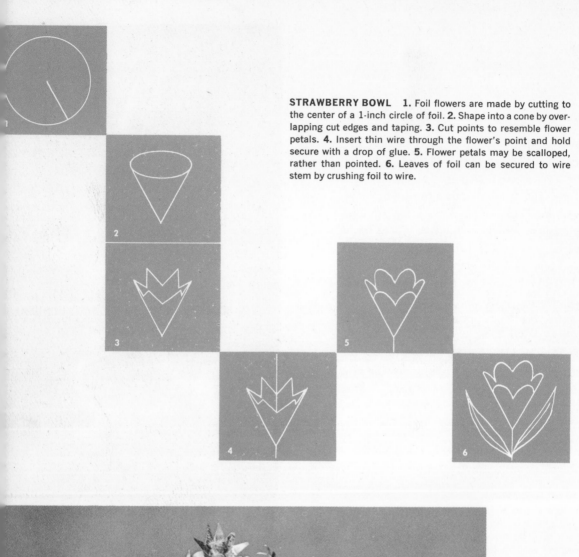

STRAWBERRY BOWL   1. Foil flowers are made by cutting to the center of a 1-inch circle of foil. **2.** Shape into a cone by overlapping cut edges and taping. **3.** Cut points to resemble flower petals. **4.** Insert thin wire through the flower's point and hold secure with a drop of glue. **5.** Flower petals may be scalloped, rather than pointed. **6.** Leaves of foil can be secured to wire stem by crushing foil to wire.

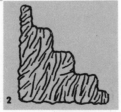

THANKSGIVING Thanksgiving is traditionally associated with the Horn of Plenty. Here is a new form for the Cornucopia to take. **1.** Pull two metal clothes hangers to form two long loops. Join hook ends together. **2.** Place one loop on flat surface, bend second loop upright. Mold and crush heavy-duty foil around both loops. Make "shelves" of crushed foil to hold fruit.

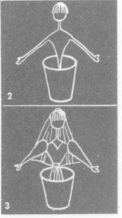

BRIDAL SHOWER Here is a delightful suggestion for a way to display all the bride-to-be's gifts at a bridal shower. And gifts like wastebaskets and mops become part of the decoration. **1.** Large wastebasket filled with gifts holds string mop upright. **2.** Give the "bride" a head (mop string provides hair) and a feminine figure of crushed foil. Arms are also crushed foil taped to the mop handle. **3.** Add a veil and dress of inexpensive net material. Artificial flowers pinned to top add color.

BRIDAL CENTERPIECE 1. As in the photograph to the right, cover large paper cups with foil. A foil-covered dowel, pencil, or candle stuck in clay or sand makes the stem. Cover an orange or foam plastic ball with foil and stick on stem. **2.** Decorate with artificial roses. As a variation, use tiny ribbon bows instead of roses. Join three together by ribbon streamers for a festive centerpiece.

Stork Shower

Since a party for a Mother-to-be is attended by her close friends, it is usually advisable to select two or three people to buy the baby gift or gifts for the entire group. This avoids duplication of gifts.

The beautiful ribbon bows on the boxes above have been attached separately so they can be taken home by the guest of honor to decorate bassinette or nursery.

Nice note: Be sure to include at least one glamorous gift for the Mother-to-be: a pretty bed jacket, cologne or perfume, or a toilet kit for her hospital stay.

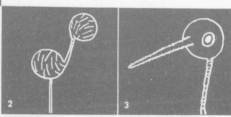

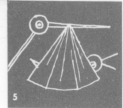

STORK SHOWER   1. Make basic bird shape, using plastic foam balls and foil (page 10). **2.** Stick foil-covered dowels or pencils in body for legs, extending foil to form feet. **3.** Curve a pipe cleaner into shape for bill. **4.** Make nest from construction-paper cylinder, topped with small Alcoa Wrap wreath (see page 26). **5.** Make smaller stork, for large stork to carry. Place storks among pile of gift packages. Use straight pins to secure stork feet to boxes. Plastic clothesline, tiny clothespins are used for extra decoration.

NEW YEAR'S EVE BUFFET Start the New Year with unusual serving pieces that can be made with ordinary household equipment, decorated with imagination.

1. Pig Cut off slice of grapefruit. Place remainder flat on dish. Cover both pieces with foil. **2.** Pin the cut slice to the front of the grapefruit. Add face features of olive slices and small meat balls. Use lemon quarters for ears.

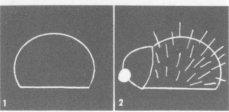

3. Swan Cover inverted oval dish with approximately 30-inch strip of foil. Leave 5 inches at end for tail, use remainder for neck and head. Turn dish over. **4.** Sweep up foil end into tail. Crush foil at other end and mold over 3-inch plastic ball for head. Cut out beak and crown (patterns page 57). Add feathers.

5. Fish Cover a flat oval serving tray with foil and shape foil edge into fish head and tail.

6. Petal Shape Mold foil over custard cup. Cut edges in rounded petal shape. Use as dish for olives and relishes.

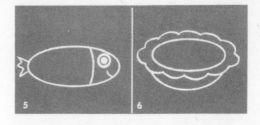

7. Flowerpot Server Foil-covered dowels are stuck into clay in flowerpot, topped with foil-covered plastic balls. Stick hors d'oeuvres on toothpicks into balls.

8. Jesters Make gay Jesters from long cones of foil gift-wrap with plastic ball heads. Pleated foil or paper collar with beads at points add color. Pin caps of crushed foil on heads.

9. Pineapple Cover pineapple with foil. Stick with small appetizers on toothpicks.

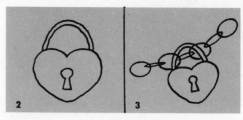

VALENTINE TREASURE CHEST This charming treasure chest can be used to contain a gift to your Valentine or as a centerpiece for your child's Pirate Party (page 38). **1.** Top a box without a lid with a piece of cardboard, curved to resemble a sea chest lid. Secure to one side of box with tape. Cover box and lid with foil and cut a slot in lid large enough for Valentine envelope. **2.** For padlock, crush foil into a heart shape and add keyhole of construction paper. Punch holes through lid. Insert U-shaped fastener for lock made from crushed foil. **3.** A chain of crushed foil links passes over the chest and through the lock. Use plastic tape fastened over lid and front of chest to simulate metal bindings.

ENGAGEMENT SHOWER 1. A crushed foil wreath (page 26) is covered with small bunches of artificial flowers. Five strips of ribbon tied to the wreath fasten it to a lighting fixture above table. **2.** Threads hang from the wreath, holding heart-shapes of construction paper and foil birds (see pattern page 57). Wings and tail are pleated foil.

BUTTERFLY TREE **1.** Cut a butterfly shape (pattern page 57) from foil and one from colored foil or construction paper. Make the colored shape smaller than the foil. Add antennae of crushed foil. Attach thin wire to each butterfly and fasten to a vine, house plant, painted driftwood or foil-covered tree branch. **2.** A butterfly makes a bright decoration for a napkin ring.

ANNIVERSARY TREE This attractive centerpiece for any anniversary is pictured to the left. **1.** Form rings of crushed foil (see front end papers). Join rings together with thread or string to form a cone. Decorate the cone of rings with artificial red roses.

PLACE MARKER **2.** Join two foil rings together with a ribbon bow.

NUMERALS **3.** Numerals of painted crushed foil in ring identify the anniversary. This "tree" can also be used as a birthday table decoration.

CHERRY TREE This easy-to-do table or buffet decoration pictured to the right is extremely adaptable. Use the tree for displaying flowers, holding gifts, or candy treats for a child's party. **1.** Cover a small branch with several layers of aluminum foil, spreading foil layers out at bottom to provide a good base for standing. Pin on cherries as pictured here. **2.** The same tree can be used in a flowerpot, hung with lollipops as treats for children.

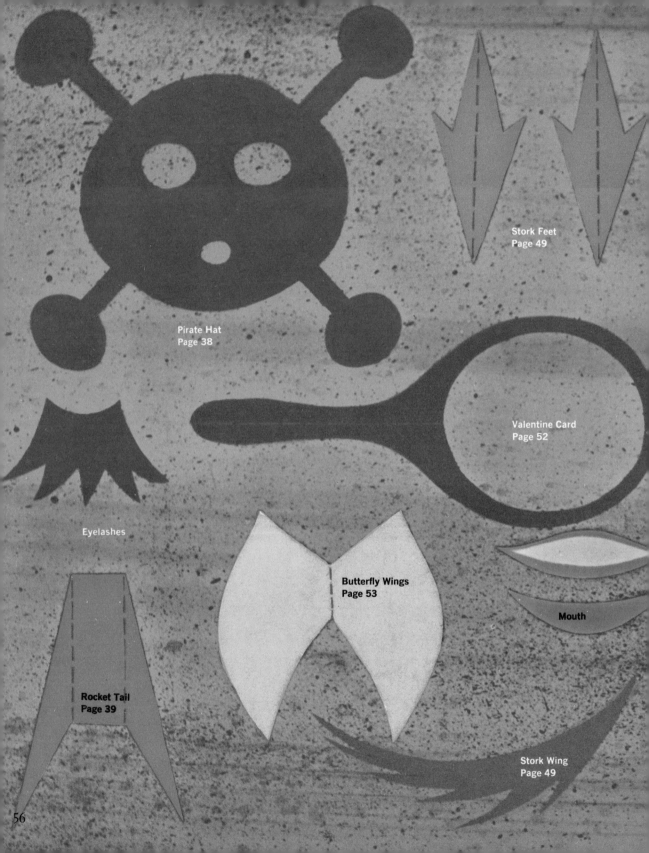

Stork Feet
Page 49

Pirate Hat
Page 38

Valentine Card
Page 52

Eyelashes

Butterfly Wings
Page 53

Mouth

Rocket Tail
Page 39

Stork Wing
Page 49

56

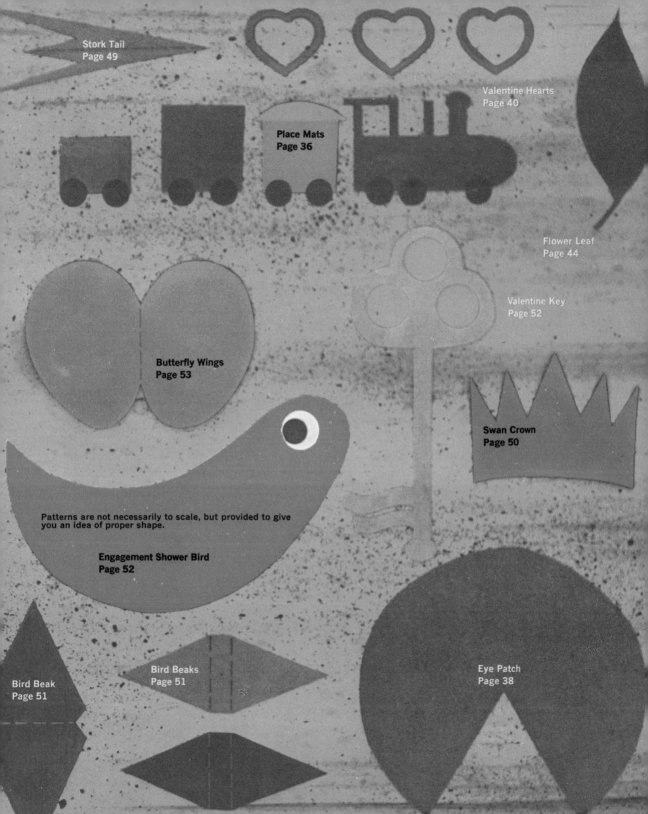

Stork Tail
Page 49

Valentine Hearts
Page 40

Place Mats
Page 36

Flower Leaf
Page 44

Valentine Key
Page 52

Butterfly Wings
Page 53

Swan Crown
Page 50

Patterns are not necessarily to scale, but provided to give you an idea of proper shape.

Engagement Shower Bird
Page 52

Bird Beaks
Page 51

Bird Beak
Page 51

Eye Patch
Page 38

Welcome to Easter

Easter is a season of beloved traditions. The Egg Tree on the opposite page is the modern version of a centuries-old design. The foil sculpture Rabbit (page 60) will be tucked into a little girl's Easter Basket by a young mother who used the same wicker basket when *she* was a little girl.

Hospitality and Open House are a part of this joyful season. Visitors are welcomed with fragrant hot coffee and trays of tender, nut-filled stollen. Let the children share in this Easter entertaining by making gift baskets and bowls (page 61) to hold candies, nuts, and jelly eggs. A simple layer cake could be transformed into an Easter Cake for the dining buffet by a Rabbit Ring, shown on page 61.

Tinted eggs, familiar symbol of the season, can be nested in a shining foil wreath like giant jewels in a silver setting. The circle wreath can be made in two minutes, following directions on page 26.

Try the wreath as a centerpiece on a dark green linen table cloth.

With a bit of glue and scraps of fabric and paper, children can turn hard-cooked eggs into droll Egg Dolls (page 67). These individual Egg Dolls can be given as gifts or used as place cards at Easter dinner.

Gift flowers and plants are a part of the Easter scene. The handsome Rooster on page 64 can be combined with sweet-smelling hyacinths or tulips as a decoration for coffee table or springtime party. For a simple, effective holder for an Easter plant, mold heavy-duty foil over the clay pot, as shown on front end papers. Flare ends of foil up over pot and cut edges in wide, even scallops.

Before you plan your next Easter program, look over the following pages for made-at-home decorations that fit the radiant spirit of Easter Sunday.

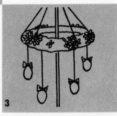

EGG TREE Your whole house takes on the gay springtime feeling of Easter with this charming lavender egg tree that can be made as one of your traditional family Easter projects. **1.** The tree is built on a full-length foil-covered broomstick. Next, an Alcoa Wrap wreath is made (page 26) 14 inches in diameter. **2.** Now take nine lavender ribbon streamers, 24 inches long, and attach to the end of the broomstick with a tack. Tie the other ends around the wreath like parasol spokes. The wreath is covered with lavender, white, and blue artificial flowers. The flowers can be held on with pins. **3.** The eggs for the tree have the insides blown out to keep them lightweight. This is easily accomplished by taking a needle and picking off a small chip of eggshell from each end of an egg. The insides are then blown into a saucer by blowing through one end. (The contents will make scrambled eggs for Easter breakfast.) After dyeing with colors, the eggs are attached to ribbon streamers 10 to 20 inches long. To attach ribbon to eggs tie knots at ends, push knots inside shells and hold with glue. Streamers are then attached evenly around the bottom of the wreath. The colorful tree will stand up if the pole is put in the center of a foil-covered flowerpot and packed in with sand or dirt. The egg tree can be made to a smaller scale for a table centerpiece using the core from an 18-inch-wide roll of foil (or 18-inch piece of wood). In this case the wreath should be about 12 inches in diameter.

Easter Baskets

There's no law that says Easter baskets must be crammed with expensive chocolate rabbits or squashy marshmallow chicks. The gay flower-bearing rabbit below will brighten any basket, later will decorate a child's table or chest of drawers. Choco-

late-covered eggs can be wrapped with foil and decorated with ribbons. Candy will remain fresh and small hands will not be smeared with melting chocolate. The easy-to-make Rabbit Bowl (below) is a holder for jelly eggs or small toy charms. Rabbit Ring, cut like paper dolls, can circle hard-cooked eggs or Easter candies. Cookies, cut into rabbit or chick shapes, are delicious additions to the basket. *Idea:* trim young girl's basket with barrettes or hair bows laced with tiny artificial flowers.

A. RABBIT BOWL A sparkling container for their Easter treat that all children will love is this rabbit bowl. Using a mixing bowl or serving dish as a mold, shape several layers of Alcoa Wrap over it to make a foil bowl (see molding instructions on front end papers). Repeat this procedure to make a duplicate bowl. **1.** Place one of these on top of the other to form the body of the rabbit. The head is made from a crushed ball of foil. **2.** Attach the head to the top half by forming a sheet of foil over it and around the top bowl shape. **3.** Pin and glue on ears (pattern page 69), eyes (page 68), a nose, and tie a ribbon bow around rabbit's neck.

EGG DECORATIONS In addition to the traditional egg dyes, there are many colorful ways to make your Easter eggs more beautiful. **1.** One way to add sparkle to an egg is to paste on the multicolored foil stars you can purchase in the 5 & 10c stores. Paste on either plain or colored eggs. **2.** Another beautiful egg decoration is achieved by wrapping the egg in a small piece of foil. Now glue on colored glitter, another 5 & 10c store material. **3.** Make striped eggs with straight or zigzag lines using crayon, dyes, water colors, or ink. **4.** Make egg faces and glue them in a collar cut from the egg carton.

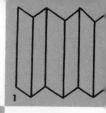

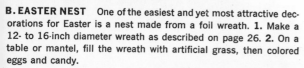

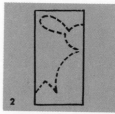

B. EASTER NEST One of the easiest and yet most attractive decorations for Easter is a nest made from a foil wreath. **1.** Make a 12- to 16-inch diameter wreath as described on page 26. **2.** On a table or mantel, fill the wreath with artificial grass, then colored eggs and candy.

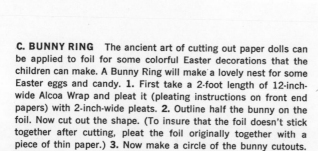

C. BUNNY RING The ancient art of cutting out paper dolls can be applied to foil for some colorful Easter decorations that the children can make. A Bunny Ring will make a lovely nest for some Easter eggs and candy. **1.** First take a 2-foot length of 12-inch-wide Alcoa Wrap and pleat it (pleating instructions on front end papers) with 2-inch-wide pleats. **2.** Outline half the bunny on the foil. Now cut out the shape. (To insure that the foil doesn't stick together after cutting, pleat the foil originally together with a piece of thin paper.) **3.** Now make a circle of the bunny cutouts. **4.** Add a circle of green construction paper. Cut in zigzag pattern to simulate grass.

D. FOIL EASTER BUNNY You can make your sparkling Easter bunny by easily molding him from foil. **1.** First crumple Alcoa Wrap into two balls, one 3 inches in diameter and another larger one 4 inches in diameter. Attach these together with glue or by running a pencil into both. **2.** Crush two 12-inch lengths (crushing instructions on front end papers) of foil for arms and for legs. Shape a ball at the ends of each crushed section for feet and hands. Also cut out 8-inch-long ears based on pattern on page 69. Now attach ears, arms, and legs with pins and glue. Add a ribbon bow around bunny's neck. Eyes, nose, and mouth are cut from colored paper and glued. Heart-shaped mouth pattern is on page 69.

ROOSTER This stylish rooster will add sparkle to Easter or to a Spring centerpiece. **1.** Cut rooster body shape from cardboard. Cover with several layers of foil. (Crushing the foil before adding to the body will add dimension.) Use section of cardboard tube from foil to make stand. Place body on top of stand, then cover entire shape with large sheet of foil. Force bottom of tube into 6-inch disc of plastic foam to make base. **2.** Glue on rooster tail and wing feathers, using actual feathers or strips of colored foil gift wrapping. Glue or pin on comb (pattern page 68) and beak (simple cone shape). Add crescent-shaped eyes.

CHICKS Have the children make these fluffy Easter chicks from yarn. Here's how. **1.** Loop the yarn around two fingers to form a full ball. Removing the loop from your fingers, tie the yarn across center with thread, making two smaller loops. Make a second yarn ball, using four fingers to produce a bigger loop than the first ball. Tie this loop through the center with thread. **2.** Place the two finished loops end to end and tie centers together with thread. Cut ends of each of the loops and fluff out into balls. These are head and body of the chick. **3.** Make chick's beak from a piece of pipe cleaner, glued onto the head. Make feet and legs from another pipe cleaner. Glue beads to head for eyes.

Egg Dolls

Gather your family around the kitchen table for an Egg Doll session. You'll find fun and excitement in this new way to decorate eggs for Easter.

You'll need a bowl of hard-cooked eggs, construction paper or plastic tape, aluminum foil, and scraps of gift-wrap paper, fabric, and ribbon.

The easiest-made Egg Dolls have bodies made from three or four inch sections of tubes from foil or paper towels.

Add a small card to the front of an Egg Doll to make a place card or Easter greeting.

Idea: No reason to limit Egg Dolls to Easter. These delightful figures could be used as a Valentine centerpiece, favors at a child's birthday party, or to top a party cake.

THE CLOWN The first in our cast of egg dolls is the clown. **1.** His head is, surprisingly enough, an egg. His body is the tube from a 12-inch-wide roll of foil. The tube is covered with foil and pushed into a disc of plastic foam which forms the base. The arms are crushed from a 12-inch length of foil with the ends of the arms shaped into hands. If you wish to keep any egg doll long, it is best to blow out its contents (page 59). **2.** The collar is made by pleating (see pleating on front end papers) a 2-inch-wide, 1-foot-long piece of colored foil gift-wrap or colored paper. Tape ends of collar together and pin or tape to body. Cut hair from foil and glue on head. **3.** The clown's hat is colored paper made into a thin cone. Clown's feet are cut from colored paper or felt (pattern page 69).

THE BABY Another of our egg doll group is our young, winsome friend, the baby who is made complete with a foil curl. **1.** The head is a blown-out egg and the body a small foil-covered cone. The point of the cone is inserted into the end of the empty egg and glued in place. **2.** Baby's bow tie is cut from colored paper and glued in place. The curl is shaped from a tightly crushed piece of foil. Ears are cut from foil. (Mouth pattern page 68.)

AND MORE Our other egg doll friends are made in similar ways. The king, the tipsy gentleman with the top hat, the robust young lady with braids, and the reclining rabbit provide other examples of the art of making egg dolls. All have cone bodies except Mr. Rabbit who is shaped from crushed foil. Patterns for many features are on pages 68 and 69.

67

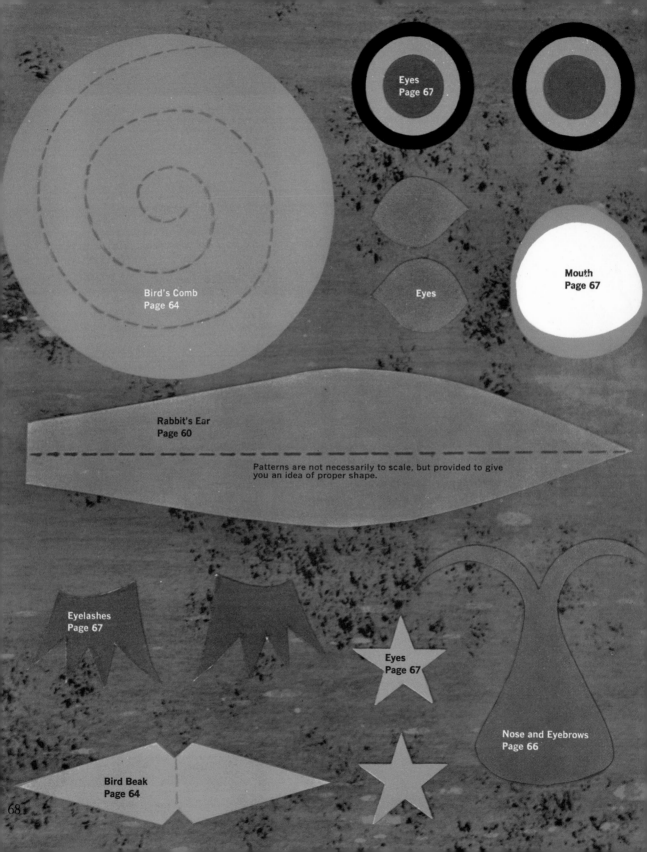

Eyes
Page 67

Bird's Comb
Page 64

Eyes

Mouth
Page 67

Rabbit's Ear
Page 60

Patterns are not necessarily to scale, but provided to give
you an idea of proper shape.

Eyelashes
Page 67

Eyes
Page 67

Nose and Eyebrows
Page 66

Bird Beak
Page 64

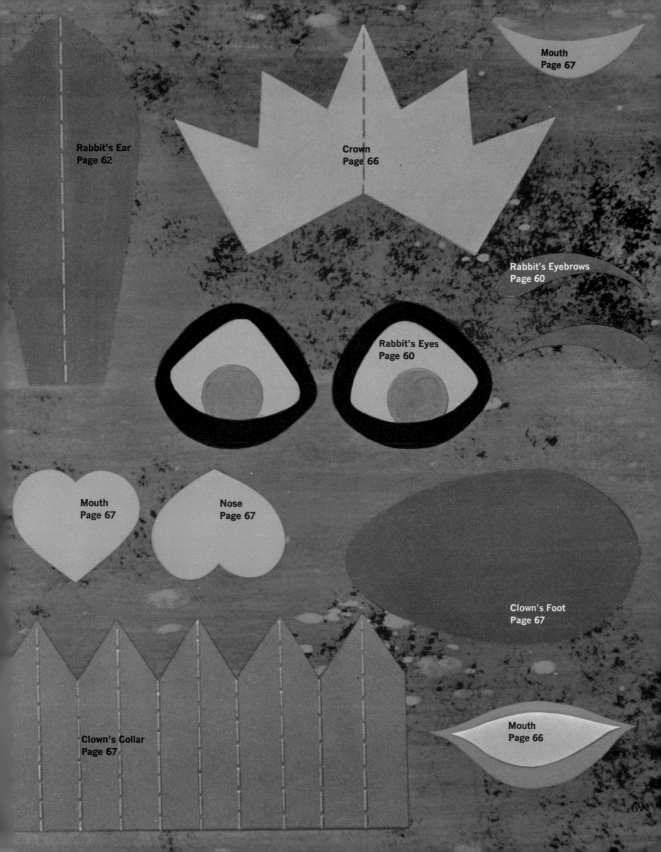

Mouth
Page 67

Rabbit's Ear
Page 62

Crown
Page 66

Rabbit's Eyebrows
Page 60

Rabbit's Eyes
Page 60

Mouth
Page 67

Nose
Page 67

Clown's Foot
Page 67

Clown's Collar
Page 67

Mouth
Page 66

Halloween Fun

Choose your favorite from an enchanting, amazing parade of foil head masks for Halloween. Here's the surprise: you can easily make one of these whimsical masks from a single roll of aluminum foil!

The masks are molded over a large balloon, the kind that sells for about 10 cents in variety stores. Shaggy hair of raffia or yarn and features of felt or construction paper add character to the masks.

These wonderful disguises slip over the head and rest on the shoulders. Since the masks cover the entire head, the children will be able to visit even their best friends without being recognized.

Let the children make their own masks. (Takes less than an hour.) Rabbits, kittens, owls and clowns are all easy to make. Robots, with foil-covered boxes for bodies, and Space Men are naturals for foil masks. Or follow a picture in a favorite book or comic strip.

As you note in the pictures, ordinary clothing can be worn with the masks—snow suits, ski suits, slacks, sweaters, heavy pajamas. This is a special advantage for young children who must be dressed warmly for their Halloween parading.

Safety note: the foil masks reflect the gleam from street lights and car headlights, especially important for youngsters walking at night.

Making masks is lively party entertainment for all ages, at any time in the year. Set a time limit for adult guests and award a prize for the best mask.

Head masks, and the wig shown on page 75, provide hours of fun for children's "dress-up" play on rainy afternoons. A big bold mask is also an unexpected and cheerful gift for any sick-in-bed youngster.

HALLOWEEN MASKS **1.** Inflate large balloon to size mask desired. For children, 10-12 inches in diameter. For adults, 12-16 inches in diameter. Tear 25-foot roll of foil into sheets 3 feet in length. (Eight sheets of foil.) Place balloon, blowing spout up, on first sheet of foil. **2.** Shape foil up around balloon. Place balloon on next sheet so foil will shape up over uncovered portion of balloon. **3.** Repeat with third sheet. **4.** Wad up one sheet of foil into ball for nose. Fasten into position with cellophane tape. **5.** Mold next sheet of foil over center of balloon and over ball, shaping to form nose. **6.** Bring remainder of foil up over balloon, smoothing neatly into place. Crimp or tuck in edges of foil at top to form head opening (7 to 9 inches in diameter). Do not tuck in edges before this step or mask will not hold together properly. Let air out of balloon and remove it from mask. **7.** Cut out eyes and mouth with scissors. Trimming directions for mask on following pages.

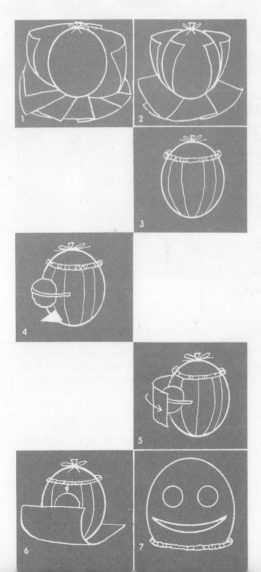

STOOPY The wistful looking fellow shown at left on page 70 is easily created with a foil mask. Use the basic instructions on page 71, but **1.** as the wad of crushed foil for his nose is added, add two more rounded wads for his fat cheeks. Then complete the mask by adding the remaining sheets of foil. **2.** Ears are shaped from double thicknesses of Alcoa Wrap and glued to head using pins to hold until glue dries. Stoopy's hair is fashioned from large loops of red ribbon. His eyes are cut out and other features are made from felt or colored plastic tape. (Eyes and mouth are suggested by patterns on pages 76 and 77.)

LION This mask, in itself, makes a truly original costume. It is made using the basic procedure described on page 71 except that **1.** when the nose is added, also add wads of crushed foil to shape the lion's chin and two cheeks. These are pieces like the nose, but not as large. After these features are added, continue shaping sheets of foil around the mask and over the features. **2.** The ears are large and rounded. They are molded from double thicknesses of foil that are crushed into the proper shape and glued on, using pins to hold. The lion's mane is made from loops of ribbon pinned in place. Lion's eyes are cut out slanted and almond-shaped. Other features are cut from felt or can be created from colored plastic tape.

CLOWN   There are endless variations of clowns that can be made with foil masks. The gay clown shown on page 70 uses the basic method of mask-making (page 71). **1.** The wad of foil for his nose is long and pointed, and an extra wad of foil is added at the same time on top of his head to give him a slightly pointed head. **2.** When the mask shape is completed, large oval eyes are cut in the mask, and a pointed hat added (this might be a party hat purchased from a 5 & 10c store). The clown's ears are molded from double-thick pieces of Alcoa Wrap and glued to the head. Loops of red ribbon are pinned on for hair. The clown's mouth and eyes, cut from cloth or made with colored plastic tape, are suggested by patterns on pages 76 and 77.

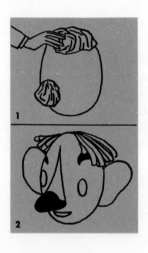

RABBIT   While a multitude of animal masks are possible with foil, one of the easiest to create is the rabbit. The wiggly-nose fellow shown here is made using the basic mask-making method (page 71). **1.** With wads of foil, during the basic steps, give this rabbit a nose and add foil to the top of his head to make it pointed. **2.** The slanted and almond-shaped eyes are suggested by patterns on pages 76 and 77. The hair is created from loops of green ribbon pinned to the mask. Ears are cut from double-thicknesses of Alcoa Wrap. Their shape is suggested by the patterns on page 76.

Halloween Tricks

Keep your scissors and roll of foil handy at Halloween for many last minute uses. Need a costume in a hurry for a small girl?

Angel robe is easily cut from an old sheet, draped and stitched into shape. For wings, cover two wire coat hangers with foil and attach to back of robe with tape slings that slip over shoulders and arms. Add halo of foil, trimmed with star.

Queen costume is same sheet robe, or white party dress, plus a crown of heavy paper covered with foil. Add a sceptre of crushed foil.

Little Bo-Peep costume is party dress, plus large flower-trimmed hat and shepherd's crook of foil. If you don't have a large picture hat, make hat of cardboard and foil. Cut out a large circle and cut head hole to fit young Bo-Peep. Cover circle with foil and decorate with artificial flowers or rosettes of gift-wrap ribbon. Secure two 3-feet ribbons to each edge of brim and tie in a big bow under chin. Make shepherd's crook by crushing together two lengths of foil, one yard long. Curve crook at top and add ribbon bow.

Neat Treat Halloweeners at the door? Serve candies, doughnuts, or popcorn in squares of foil, twisted at the top to seal.

Cowboy Stuff If your young son dresses as his favorite cowboy for Halloween, add a dashing horse to his outfit. Make horse on broomstick or mop handle, following directions given on page 33. Western note: foil-covered cardboard makes impressive Sheriff's badge for young heroes.

Fortune Apples Type out fortune on slip of paper, fold in small section of foil. Make slit in side of apple and insert fortune. Use Fortune Apples as favors, fastening by ribbons to Jack-o'-Lantern centerpiece.

Halloween Animals Use basic animal directions given on page 82 to make spooky cats and owls for Halloween favors and decorations.

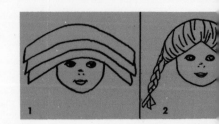

PIGTAIL WIG 1. Place three sheets of foil, measuring about 36 inches long, on top of head. 2. Hold foil steady on head with palm of hand. Mold foil down over head, tucking in edges around face. Crush ends of foil into long tight ropes and braid into pigtails. 3. Tie large bow on each braid.

EASY-TO-MAKE WIGS Foil makes inexpensive wigs for Halloween costumes, parties, or amateur plays. The wigs are shaped right on the head. Have an assistant handy to help with the first steps.

Face Masks Complete the Costume

No need to shop the stores for that very special mask needed to complete a costume. With a roll of aluminum foil and a few snippings of ribbon and paper, you can custom-make a mask for your Halloween outfit.

FACE MASKS Note the basic shape of the masks shown on this page, then trace and cut out mask from heavy-duty foil. Make mask long enough to extend about 1 inch past the chin and about 2 inches past the top of the head. Cut three slits, 1½ inches long, in top of mask; one slit at center, other slits half-way between center and edge of mask. This allows mask top to be bent and molded over top of forehead, curving sides of mask. Cut out eyes, nose, and mouth openings. Trim edges smooth. Decorate around features with colored paper, crayons, poster paint, or felt-tipped colored markers. Glue ribbon or heavy tape to sides. Now for the touches that add fun to the face masks. **Curls** are 1-inch strips of foil, curled over pencil or candle and glued to top of mask. **Beard** can be made from double-fold of foil, about 10 inches long, crushed to pointed shape. Glue to mask under the mouth. **Mustache** is 6-inch strip of crushed foil, pinched at center and turned up at each end. Glue under nose.

HALF-MASKS Cut half-masks or Harlequin masks from heavy-duty foil. Cat mask is cut down to mouth, with opening for nose. Outline eyes with crayon, paint, or colored paper. Glue on thin strips of foil for cat's whiskers.

MASKS FOR DECORATIONS These daffy, delightful foil faces, resembling Mexican carnival masks, also make spectacular Halloween decorations. Place several masks in the window, lighted from behind with lamp or light bulb. Extra-large masks can be used as table centerpiece or to decorate a door.

Patterns are not necessarily to scale, but provided to give you an idea of proper shape. Sketch the outline from the pattern first, then cut out.

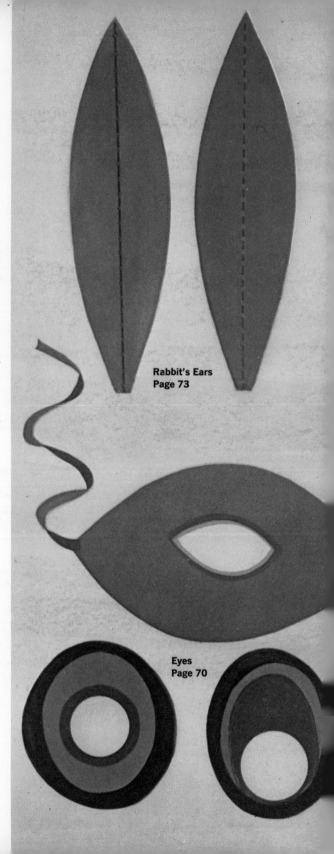

Rabbit's Ears
Page 73

Eyes
Page 70

Eye
Page 73

Eye
Page 72

Mouth
Page 70

Mouth
Pages 70 and 73

77

Fanciful Thing

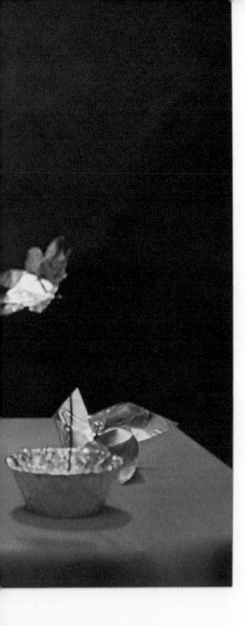

In the golden years of childhood, to "make something" is as natural to a youngster as to eat, run, or laugh. Every child needs encouragement to keep this joyful creativeness alive. This assistance can be as simple as keeping plenty of art material at hand and showing appreciation of the final work. Appreciation is the fine point here: not a casual "very nice" before returning to the evening newspaper or the dinner dishes, but a few precious minutes to look at a foil ladybug or flower, and to understand.

All these designs have something of magic in them. We hold a sheet of foil in our hands; in minutes, with a few twists of the fingers, the shining sheet becomes a bird or a glistening tree.

This is our all-ages, all-talents, let's-have-fun section, crammed with ideas that slip naturally into everyday living.

The young daughter across the page, for instance, is taking her first step toward being a grown-up hostess by molding shiny flower pots and blossoms for a table centerpiece.

All the ideas on the following pages, including the puppet theatre, are fine rainy day or sickroom projects. If you have a baby sitter in the house, she'll find ideas for keeping children happy and busy.

And consider this as a gift section, too. All of these art projects would be inexpensive, attractive gifts for a child to make and give. What fond grandmother wouldn't welcome her very own Lion!

for All

PINWHEEL Pinwheels for spinning in the breeze can be fun! Those convenient foil plates that so many frozen foods are packaged in these days are all you need. **1.** Cut a pie plate into a square, then cut in toward the center from each of the four points. Stop each cut about ½ inch from the center. **2.** Now, fold each point over to the center and pin on a wooden dowel. A thumbtack works fine and will allow the pinwheel to turn. **3.** The finished pinwheel looks like this.

Foil Sculpture

This book introduces a fascinating new craft: sculpturing in aluminum foil.

All ages and talents can enjoy this activity. It is inexpensive and simple to do.

Foil sculpture needs nothing but the foil itself, plus a few trimmings. Sheets of ordinary aluminum foil are crushed between the hands, then molded into shape. After the basic figure is formed, additional sheets of foil are layered over the foundation shape to make the finished product. Objects of molded foil can be manipulated into various positions without bending or breaking.

Since foil is extremely pliable, sections can be twisted, pinched, cupped, and rolled into a variety of shapes. For very large figures that have to remain erect, skeletons of wire are used to set shape and size, then padded with foil.

Projects in foil sculpture can be as simple as the ladybug on page 84 or as elaborate as the Mermaid on page 90. All the animals and figures in this section have been molded of foil. The same three-dimensional technique can produce dolls, trees, and relief maps.

Take matters in your own hands and make a bold start with the directions on page 82. As soon as you get the feel of the work, experiment with your own ideas and designs.

MELVIN MOUSE A gay toy or room decoration. Also makes a lively centerpiece at a child's party. **1.** Cover a small sprinkling can—the kind Mother uses to sprinkle her ironing—with foil. Mold foil over a small plastic sugar scoop and stick the handle into the sprinkler opening. **2.** Decorate the scoop with features of felt, colored paper, and yarn. Use ovals of paper or felt for feet. A long, thin strip of fabric or paper is glued to the bottom of the can for a tail. Crushed foil arms are taped to the back of the mouse and curved around to the front.

PUPPETS AND PUPPET STAGE   Puppets are fun. And a puppet stage for back-yard or basement shows is easy to make. Cut out one side of a cardboard box to produce a three-sided stage. Cut out an opening in the opposite side for a stage. The top flap attached to the side to be used as the stage should remain. Cut off other flaps. Pull remaining box flap upright and cut into a curve. Cover entire box and upright flap with foil.

PUPPETS   Long handled wooden spoons or wooden dowels make good puppet bodies. Stick on a plastic foam ball or ball of crushed foil for a head. A square of fabric with a hole in the center is slipped on the stick to complete the puppet. Use felt, buttons, beads, construction paper for features and trim for the puppets.

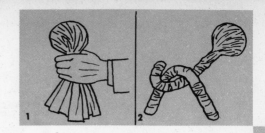

Conny's Zoo

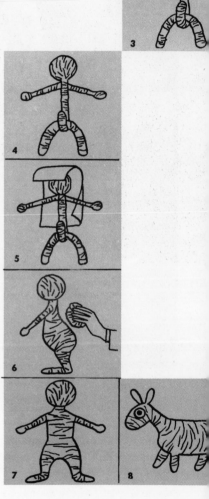

Follow the arrows to Miss Conny's Zoo
If you're looking for animals playful and new.
On the following pages, we're sure you will find
Some beasts of a _most_ unusual kind:
A dazzling blonde lion with hair up in bows
A stylish young bear with a blue flannel nose
Two shy, charming storks with pipe cleaner bills
Two mad Lulu Birds sporting red feather quills.
Who is the keeper of this zooper zoo?
Here's the best part—it can easily be you!
So read the directions, then work with a vigor
And watch your own zoo get bigger and bigger.

BASIC ANIMAL SHAPE **1.** Crush a 3-foot length of foil to form head and body. **2.** Crush an 18-inch piece of foil and bend in half over first piece, about 3/4 of the way from the head end. **3.** Fold body portion over leg piece to hold in place. **4.** Another 18-inch sheet of foil is crushed to form arms. **5.** A sheet of foil molded over the head and down the back holds the arm section in place. **6.** Add sheets of foil to form various parts of the body. Crush foil lightly until a definite shape is formed. **7.** The basic figure is now formed—head, body, arms, and legs. **8.** By bending figure over, it becomes a dog, horse, cat, etc. Sculpture foil to make distinguishing features for each type of figure.

LION A bold, but kindly lion can be a playmate, a room decoration, or a party highlight. **1.** Start with the basic animal figure described on page 82. Bend the figure into a sitting position with front legs touching the floor or tabletop. **2.** Build up the body with several layers of foil. **3.** One of the sheets of foil is crushed to form a tail. Mold foil head to form lion's face, and add foil ears (pinned or glued). Loops of ribbon glued or pinned to the head make the mane, and eyes and nose are cut from felt or colored paper and glued to the face.

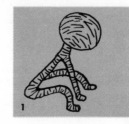

LADYBUG   A bright ladybug is a fun-project for young hands. **1.** Cut a foam ball in two, one piece larger than the other. Cover both pieces with foil. **2.** Pin the smaller piece on the front of the larger. Black pipe cleaners are used for antennae. **3.** A circle of red construction paper, with a small wedge shape cut out, becomes the back and wings. Glue on black dots of colored paper or felt. **4.** Glue entire construction paper back to the top of the bug. Add a black bead to the head portion for a nose.

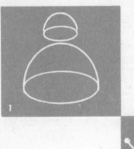

SMALL ANIMAL PROJECTS Here is a delightful group of animal friends to be made by young hands. Left to right: **1.** Make the storks by beginning with the basic bird shape shown in the Christmas decoration section. Make the necks longer, however, and omit tail. Punch a hole in the bottom of the foam ball that forms the body and insert a drinking straw. Mold feet of foil to ends of the straws. Colored pipe cleaner pieces make the tails and beaks. **2.** The bear is made of two foam balls, placed one atop the other. Cover both with foil. Add more foil to the top ball and mold into bear features. Crush foil into arm and leg shapes, hold to the body shape, and cover with additional foil to hold in place. Form ears from crushed foil, make indentations in either side of foam ball head with thumbnail and insert edges of ears. Add face features of construction paper or felt. **3.** The tall giraffe is made of two tiny foam balls and one a trifle

larger. One is used for the body, and the other two for the head. Crush foil around two smaller balls for the head, bring foil down and crush for a neck. Wrap remainder of foil sheet around the third foam ball. Add more foil to the body to make thicker. Crush two lengths of foil about 8 inches long and drape each over top of body form for the legs. Add more foil to the body, covering the legs to hold secure. Mold the head with the fingers. Markings are made from construction paper or felt. **4.** Two foam balls are used for the basis of the camel. Cover small one with foil for the head, molding foil into a head shape. Bring foil down to form the neck and cover the second foam ball for the body. Add more foil for the hump and drape two pieces of crushed foil over the body for the legs. Add more foil to hold legs secure and to fill out body shape. Use paper or felt for face features. Use also at Christmas with the Three Wise Men (pages 20-21).

1   2   3   4

BALLERINA OSTRICH (See cover.) **1.** Mold the basic bird shape described below. Use larger sheets of Alcoa Wrap to make the long legs and long neck. **2.** Add face features of colored felt or paper. Feathers are inserted in holes punched into the foil body. A few drops of glue in each hole will hold feathers securely. Cover feet and wind ribbon around legs for ballet slippers.

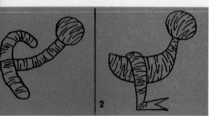

LULU BIRDS These gay creatures add fun to any party or table setting. **1.** Crush a 3-foot length of foil and shape into head and body. Drape sheet of foil over body and extend down to form long legs. **2.** Hold legs in place with another wrapping of foil and flatten ends of legs into feet. **3.** Add more foil to build up body, sculpturing into shape. **4.** Punch holes into each side of foil body, slanting punches toward the head.   Drop a little glue into each hole and insert bright-colored feathers. Add features.

BEARS 1. Make basic animal shape (page 82), adding extra foil to fatten the body. Mold the head into a bear face. Add foil ears. Make face features of felt or construction paper. **2.** Add hair of yarn or strips of felt. Add a paper or fabric dress to one bear, a terry cloth front to the other.

ELEPHANT 1. A basic animal shape (page 82) is the start for these appealing elephants. Fatten the body with additional layers of foil and add a crushed foil trunk and a tail. **2.** Add enough foil to make the head and body and mold the foil to the proper shape. **3.** Pin large foil elephant ears to the sides of the head. Add features to head, ears, and trunk with felt or construction paper. Decorate animal with spray paint.

Fun for a Large Party

The soulful mermaid across the way will soon be settled on the bandstand in a ballroom. Surrounded by dancing couples, she'll be the dazzling decoration at an Under-the-Sea Ball in New Orleans.

On the following pages, you'll see photographs of the actual Ball, along with pictures from two other successful parties: a Children's Animal Party and a City Skyline Ball. The unusual backgrounds and details could be adapted to any club, high school, sorority, or college party.

Foil for Large-Scale Decorations

All these parties were decorated with aluminum foil. The committees selected foil because it was inexpensive, flame-proof, easily obtained, and simple enough to be handled by amateur decorators.

They discovered it could be molded over chicken wire or cardboard foundations without nailing and could be painted, sprayed, and lacquered with spectacular effects.

Tips for Decorations Committees

Select a theme for even the simplest party. Plan one or two bold main decorations easily seen in even a crowded room.

Trimmings always take longer than planned. Make them in advance (like our water sprite here) and put into place the day of decorating.

Include these three members on your committee: an artistic type to sketch design, a handyman to supervise construction, a practical type to budget and buy materials.

UNDER-THE-SEA SETTING Transform gym, club, or ballroom into an underwater grotto, complete with mermaids, fish, octopus. Time bonus: fish, coral, mermaids can be made at home days before party. Fish and octopus are molded over balloons in same technique as Halloween Masks (page 71). Large foil fish can cover lighting fixtures. **Mermaid** is molded on skeleton of wire. (See foil sculpture on page 80.) Hair is raffia, tail covered with green fish netting. Rocks and grottoes are chicken wire foundation, covered with heavy-duty aluminum foil and sprayed with paint. Interesting props: boat lanterns, diving suits, heavy nets and floats, snorkels.

SKYLINE BALL Create skyline of your city or campus for party background. Or dramatize outline of two or three familiar buildings. Cut building outlines from sheets of heavy corrugated cardboard. Cover with foil, fastening to back of cardboard with cellophane tape. If buildings are large, brace back with wooden strips. Cut out windows and fill openings with strips of colored gelatin paper from art store. Light windows from behind for interesting effect. Hang foil stars from ceiling for sky. Add props of plywood or cardboard covered with foil and decorated with paint: trolley cars, college landmarks, trees, traffic lights, street signs, store fronts. **Idea:** familiar signs and sights add charm. Visit merchants, TV and radio stations for posters, signs, trade marks.

CHILDREN'S ANIMAL PARTY Delightful theme for church bazaar, children's party, kindergarten festival. Center of attraction is **Wishing Tree.** Make trunk from cylinder of chicken wire, eight inches in diameter. Branches are long lengths of crushed heavy-duty foil, stuck into top of chicken wire trunk. Lace branches with heavy cord or thin wire and fasten to ceiling in criss-cross pattern. Cover wire trunk with foil and spray with brown paint. Fasten small favors and ribbon bows to branches. (Small trees can also be made, using tube from rolls of foil for trunk.) For **Animals,** trace and cut outlines of elephant, kangaroo, giraffe from heavy cardboard. Brace large shapes in back with thin wooden strips. Give shape to animals by crumpling sheets of foil and stapling to head, arms, legs. Cover with smooth foil and tape to back. Use paint or plastic tape for features. **Elephant:** reinforce trunk with flexible wire, turn up at end so animal can be used for ring toss game. **Kangaroo:** for pouch, fasten plastic wastebasket to front of figure with strip of striped fabric. Use for bean bag game.

For further information on use of foil for dance or large party decorations, plus special large quantity packages of Alcoa Wrap, write to: Dance Decorations, Aluminum Company of America, 1501 Alcoa Building, Pittsburgh 19, Pennsylvania.

Balloons

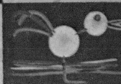

Pipe Cleaners

MATERIALS FOR YOUR DECORATIONS

The decorations in this book were designed to be made easily from materials that are easy to get. Nothing is more frustrating than to set out to make something and then discover that you can't finish it because you don't have a particular material to complete it. For this reason, should this book inspire you to create, make certain you have everything you need before you begin.

Practically everything in ALCOA'S BOOK OF DECORATIONS can be made with materials shown on these endpapers. Specifically they are:

ALUMINUM FOIL One of the most versatile materials for any decorations is aluminum foil. It can be purchased in supermarkets and department stores in regular weight in 12-inch and 8-inch widths and in heavy-duty weight in 18-inch and 12-inch widths. Rigid foil plates are also versatile for making decorations.

TAPE Clear cellophane tape and the colored plastic tapes are invaluable for making an endless number of things.

BALLOONS From your local 5 & 10c store.

PIPE CLEANERS From the hobby shop, 5 & 10c store, or tobacco counter.

PAPER Colored construction paper or drawing paper.

RIBBON Inexpensive ribbons in all colors are available in every 5 & 10c store.

PLASTIC FOAM Plastic foam shapes are available in 5 & 10c stores and in most variety or hobby shops. They come in balls, discs, slabs and sticks and can easily be cut to other shapes with knife or razor.

BOTTLES Of all shapes and sizes.

PAINT Foil can be painted with poster paints, enamels, and lacquers (avoid only simple water colors).

FLOWERS Artificial and natural.

GLUE For foil, white glues like Elmer's Glue-All are recommended.

Plastic Foam

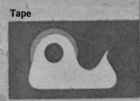

Tape

Ribbon

Bottles

Glasses

Flowers

Candles

Glue

Scissors and Thread

ALCOA WRAP

Spoons

Fruit

Paint